T0065184

TURNER
and the
BEAR

TURNER
and the
BEAR

Sheriff Turner

M.E. BLAZIC

Archway Publishing books may be ordered through booksellers or by contacting:

Archway Publishing
1663 Liberty Drive
Bloomington, IN 47403
www.archwaypublishing.com
844-669-3957

ISBN: 978-1-6657-4952-7 (sc)
ISBN: 978-1-6657-4951-0 (e)

Library of Congress Control Number: 2023916602

Print information available on the last page.

Archway Publishing rev. date: 09/05/2023

Inspired by a man of many talents,
Anthony Hopkins.

For
Lorry Paris
August 1947-March 2012
And
Red Dog (Boutros)
November 1996 – November 2011

Dedication
For all Law Enforcement Officers, especially their
K9 units; who go without a whisper for us.

Acknowledgements
San Bernardino County Sheriff Department,
San Bernardino Police Department,
Los Angeles Police Department,
California Highway Patrol,
For all of their hard work training
police K9's; for without them,
many of us would not be here today.
National Teton Forest Rangers,
Yellowstone Forest Rangers,
Utah Forestry Service and the State Police for their bravery.

Veterinarians
Dr. Jamie Velasco, DVM.
Dr. Kim, DVM
Dr. James Hudson, DVM

Also a special thanks to General Motors
Corporation for making the legendary
Chevy Silverado 4X4.

Names have been changed for privacy.

M. E. Blazic
12 June, 2012

ONE

It was a warm refreshing day in Big Bear Valley, California; the monsoon season had finally passed and Turner lay stretched out across his heavy quilt snoring while he slept peacefully. In the small cabin his retired partner and best friend Mare was fixing him dinner. An occasional sound of a squirrel or two passing over the roof would catch Turners attention, but nothing moved Turner unless he wanted to move. Being an English Bull Massif and part Bordeaux Turner was a massive animal. His face similar to that of a grizzly bear, his mask alone said a thousand words; and with a brindle pattern for his coat, he was beyond scary, especially weighing in at 165 pounds. Many people would say, "My, isn't he a looker" or "Can you imagine seeing him run after you in a chase?" Many criminals did experience this and boy did they run. Like an Elk, he could leap up and be on you like a fly. Unfortunately, Turner had his own issues to deal with; he was not able to complete the Sherriff's training academy due to medical complications. So for the last three years the quilt had become his resting place. He was now five and half years old and like a huge paperweight, unmovable, last mine.

One particular characteristic about Turner that surprised many people was his speedy movement when he decided to get up; he was quick as lightning during a tumultuous storm. No one could ever catch this dog except for his partner, Mare, who would simply sing his song and suddenly he would appear staring with his smoky bear eyes directly into hers while she continued to sing. Turner had everyone buffaloed; he could be a scary guy. He was such a nice and gentle dog to most, but Mare, knowing him could only smile and think, they don't know him like I do. Sure, he's a really nice guy, big and friendly, a big ham.

Mare put down his bowl of food, then as usual, he smelled the food and in one swallow the food disappeared into his parts unknown. Then he would snort like a bear as bubbles of drool oozed from his mouth in pure contentment. Quickly he would happily retreat back to his quilt just to go back to sleep and begin his never-ending snoring while his eyes remained opened. Turner had become just plain lazy and fat. Everyday around eleven thirty in the morning, Turner would walk Mare to the Sugarloaf post office, even in the winter months when there is lots of ice and snow on the ground. He loved the cold months and was crazy about snow and the below zero temperatures. Turner would roll in the snow, eat it, and then eventually bury himself in it as well. For him this was a wonderful time to be alive.

During the winter months when the snow was piled high along the streets and fences, the walk to the post office would more often than not turn out to be a scary adventure. Dogs in the neighborhood were able to jump their fences and charge Turner and Mare while they were on their walk. Turner is usually a friendly animal towards other animals but when the other dog would try to attack, Turner would open his huge mouth, putting it completely over the other dogs head and clamp down. The shock of this would send the other dog running frantically away leaving Turner and Mare unharmed. This act was Turners way of saying "no way buddy, take it back to your own door". Mare would just watch and laugh. People would get scared of Turner and told her so; she would reply that her dog is on a leash while theirs are running loose; which by the way was a violation of State and City laws. Most people would retreat to their homes without another word to Mare. However, there were some individuals that would pursue the matter to no avail and always lost; that's how the law works.

During the summer, life was somewhat more difficult for him. He could not take the heat and would often faint or lie down in the street when he was overheated. Mare would patiently wait with him while he recovered from the exhaustion due to the hot temperatures. This was one of several contributing factors to why he did not complete his sheriff training. He could catch the bad guy without any problems but when he was done the sheriff department would need a crane or around eight officers to lift him out of the street because he would lay there with his feet straight up in the air like he was dead because he had fainted from exhaustion. It truly was a sight to see, one would have to see it to believe it. Now, three years later, retired Sheriff Turner, lies on his quilt in his quiet cabin, just like a huge, unmovable, paperweight.

Mare was a rather petite figured blonde woman, and when she, to her great surprise, received a large amount of settlement money, fluffed her hair back and began planning an adventure for Turner and herself in her Chevy Silverado 4x4 pickup truck. She kept on saying that she and Turner would be traveling the world renowned and doing well for themselves. The day came to leave and Turners best friend, a 12 pound Chihuahua named Deputy Taz, came to say goodbye. Taz was tan with stocky legs front and rear. He thought he was the king of Sugarloaf; nothing got past Taz or got away from him. Mare heard the Taz bellow, but while he bellowed he would choke up and his owner Jon would have to rub his neck till he calmed down. Taz was not fixed so whenever female dogs passed by he thought they belonged only to him and on one else. Often enough Taz would even sneak out of his yard to come visit Turner, and Mare never did get used to his pop in visits. He would walk right in the front door of the cabin and proceed to where Turner was sleeping only get receive a snort from Turner that would startle Taz enough to quickly retreat back out. Today, Turner and Taz ran towards each other like brothers in the middle of the street. A huge hug was definitely their goal. As they met Taz would stand up on his hind legs, gently cock his head to the side and nestle into Turners neck. Turner would also turn his head and a hug emerged. Once Turner was lifted into the back of the truck with the help of Jon, who was six feet six inches tall and rather slender with the longest braid of blonde hair ever imagined, Turner and Mare began their journey.

TWO

WITH FRIENDS WAVING GOODBYES AND THROWING HUGS, TURNER laid down in the rear of Mare's truck. For a while he was comfortable until they reached the bottom of the mountain. The temperature began to rise and the heat started to take its toll on his body. Mare's first stop was at a truck stop in Jean, Nevada. The heat there was intense as the temperature read 111 degrees. Mare had to bring Turner bags of ice to pour in his five gallon bucket of water. After cooling him down and reloading him they were once again traveling. After many hours of driving the heat again overtook Turner and Mare had to get a motel room in St. George, Utah. Turner quickly found the coolest place to lie down and that was under a large tree near the pool and Jacuzzi. Once again he became like an unmovable paperweight, even while the hot wind continually blew. While Mare swam, she kept a close eye on Turner; people kept admiring him and mentioning how he resembled a grizzly bear. Turner not taking note of all of the attention seemed more focused on blending into the green grass and relaxing as much as he could. Mare's petite figure, blonde hair, and old school tattoos attracted many looks, she did not care. At 62 years old and having spent 47 years as a truck driver and law enforcement officer, she thought that the looks she received were not important because that was another place, another time, in the very distant past. This pair, Turner the Burner and Mare, was enough for anyone.

As the sun set Turner was ready for dinner, now rested they went to their room. Mare fed him his regular food and like normal he would smell it, devour it in one bite, and the bubbles would ooze out displaying his contentment while he retreated back to second bed full of pillows for comfort and began snoring away, eyes wide open. Mare decided to walk over to the local restaurant and brought back her dinner as well as some goodies for Turner.

After a goodnights sleep, the first problem of the day was how to get Turner back into the rear of the truck. He was so large that Mare could not lift him. Mare eyed three huge rocks almost high enough for Turner to stand on then step into the truck. She also noticed two gardeners, she thought maybe if she gave those guys five dollars each, they would assist her with lifting Turner back into the truck. She reversed the truck and backed up to the large rocks; the gardeners helped her get the massive dog back into the vehicle and once again they were back on the road enjoying their adventure.

THREE

As the temperature increased to 105 degrees, Mare decided to take another road leading into Utah's National Forest. Hopefully the temperature would decrease as Turner was feeling the heat again and was not doing very well. They took many breaks along the way; the country was so beautiful they just wanted to enjoy every moment of it that they could. Soon nightfall came and Mare found herself on a road she was not familiar with. All of the campgrounds were full. Mare continued driving, she finally came upon a parking lot along the river with picnic tables, restrooms, and eerily lots of police tape wrapped around the entire area. Mare thought of the police tape and how the Sheriff K9's including Turner, stole it from one of the training rooms chewing it up like bubble gum and having scattered it everywhere. After parking, Mare cut the tape and walked Turner to the river which was moving very fast like rapids. They stood back from the edge to take in the sight of the rapidly moving water and after they walked a little further ate dinner and bedded down for the night. There was no one else there, probably because of the police tape.

About 1:00 am in the morning a bright light was on her truck; it was the Utah state police shining their spotlight. They were just checking on them to make sure they were ok. Turner growled and Mare waived; the police blinked their lights and left. Mare thought how nice that was for them to check in and make sure everyone was safe. Especially since no one else was there, probably because of the police tape. Mare had a sticker on her ride side windshield; Fraternal Order of Police - State of California with a five pointed star, 2006 active supporter it read. Yes she was an active supporter of law enforcement. The next morning they awoke to much cooler weather, they had travelled all the way to the mountains. Mare had no idea where they were, so after breakfast they started off again. First stop was a mini mart along the way to get directions to Yellowstone National Forest where they planned to camp for several days.

FOUR

It was now nearing the second week of July, 2011. It was much cooler since the snow had melted so late. After another rests and finding help to lift Turner back in the truck away they went to Yellowstone, Wyoming. They finally arrived at the National Teton Forest. Mare decided to stay there for the night. Camping at Coulder Bay, they had all the supplies she thought they would need. Finally settled for the night Turner fell asleep quickly. Sleep finally took over Mare as she had been thinking about all of the activities that had been going on recently. The next day arrived with a beautiful dawn awakening. Turner was anxious to get out and do his duties and check out this great new forest they were in. Mare quickly let him out and she prepared her usual tea. Sipping her tea she read some leaflets about all of the activities to participate in her in the forest, for example, kayaking, canoeing, horseback riding, and or course hiking the trails. Wonderful she thought. But then she had a thought of what to do with Turner while she was out having fun? The Rangers quickly advised her that there were no kennels or veterinarians in the area; the closest facility was fifty miles back in Jackson Hole, Wyoming. Mare torked a wee bit, what did they mean there were no facility for animals? Is this not her world's greatest animal forest? And there are no kennels or veterinarians on the grounds? Mare like Turner was burning; this was very unacceptable to her. People came from all over the world to visit Yellowstone and the National Teton Forest. Mare eventually settled down and went to the campground mini-mart. She washed some clothes there and bought some more supplies while finishing up some letters she had to write. Meanwhile Turner lay under the trees along the side of the steps asleep and snoring continuously. The area was fenced with steel poles for the stairs; people passed by him unnoticed. Then it happened! A lady screamed in terror. Mare came running out as did everyone else. Turner stood up. It's a bear, a bear, a bear! She ran off as did five or six others. Mare yelled, "Wait! It's only a big dog", but they never heard her. The rangers came and asked Mare why she tethered her dog there? She told them that the lady who was in charge of the camp ground had told her it was ok to tether him there. The rangers looked back down at Turner and he was already snoring again. The rangers agreed that he was fine there but were surprised at his similarity to that of a bear. Everyone eyed Turner as they passed, he just kept on snoring. What was his motto?

Mare and Turner returned to their campsite. Turner anxious to lay in the shade of the trees became slightly aggressive. She pulled into the campsite quickly letting Turner out on his boot paws. Mare was still worried about Turners health, he was so big and still concerned if this trip was too much for him to handle. He rested under a large tree. Other dogs had visited this area while they were out and people walking their animals nearby quickly retreated to their own areas because they were intimidated by Turner. A Cockapoodle on a leash, a gray pit bull, a black Labrador, and lastly even a few cats were quickly escorted away. Mare just smiled.

The afternoon sun was slowly disappearing and the clouds seemed to be gathering very quickly. Lightning cracked in the sky! Turner moved so fast it was as if the lightning had struck him. Mare just laughed because she thought it was a funny reaction. Very quickly though it wasn't funny anymore; Turner was in a frantic state trying to get back into the truck. Mare lifted him with her right knee and both arms. Hail and thunder began to rule the forest. The storm lasted thirty minutes, but while the storm roared Turner growled and drooled large bubbles; nothing like a raging storm to arouse the best in him. He was always ready for anything. Now that the storm passed all was quiet and he quickly went back to his comfort spot near the large trees.

FIVE

BEFORE DARK SET IN MARE DECIDED TO TAKE TURNER FOR A WALK and also get a layout of the campground. More campers had arrived by now and most recognized Turner for a big lazy dog. Mare just laughed to herself, thinking yep, a big lazy dog he is. Young children came up to pet him and their parents were amazed at his kindness and gentility towards others. Polite conversation now took place and mostly Mare was asked about his breed. It was a pleasant time. As they continued their walk, they saw lots of squirrels and chipmunks; similar to Alaska but not as heavily populated. They also saw a few deer but no bears, elk, or other large animals nearby. Night was coming quickly so they headed back to settle down for the evening. The park rangers made their rounds as usual and warned people to be bear aware. The big bears and other large animals were just now coming down off the high peaks and mountains because the snow had melted so late in the season. Mare thought its July 15th, the animals were usually already out earlier in the year.

In Big Bear the bears come out in March. There once was a

mother bear with three cubs that sat in the middle of the street around midnight. Charlton, my neighbor and Taz's house sitter came out that evening and saw the mother bear sitting along with her babies. The bear sat straight up and looked at him; he quickly stepped back into the door. She dropped to her paws and the four bears continued down the street towards the Fire department where the large trash bin was located. This really scared Charlton something fierce; being a rather large man he still knew the fear of a mother bear with her cubs.

The rangers told the campers about a mother grizzly who had cubs plus a daughter who had two cubs of her own. They advised the campers of bear safety awareness since these bears had been recently spotted in the area of the campground. Mare listened to their warnings and wrote down the bear tag numbers just in case. Mare chuckled a bit, been here two days, almost three and haven't seen one yet she thought.

She thought about the grizzlies in Alaska. The biggest she had ever seen was about eighteen hundred pounds. She thought a bear that size must stand at least seven or eight feet tall. At the time of the encounter she could tell it was a female and she was not real aggressive either. Mare had been looking for one of her sled dogs and ended up in grizzly bait area. She came across a fifty five gallon drum loaded down with last year's meat atop of it and a tall post for the hunter to sit on, to stalk and wait for a bear. A horrible thought always passed through her when one waits for the kill of any animal.

It had been a really long day; after the rangers left, Mare and Turner ate dinner. They had been out seeing all of the wonderful activities that Mare could have done but could not

do with Turner. Especially without a dog kennel available. Mare
sarcastically thought 'some kind of wonderful this is'. So as
night shadowed in gently so did Mare and Turner. Turner as
usual fell asleep quite quickly, completely exhausted. Around 10
pm Turner did his usual howling; it was a deep loud low howl.
Massifs are known for howling in their sleep. First time Mare
heard it she thought a wolf or a bear was in her son in laws home.
Hah! It was just Turner. He would go on for about five minutes
and sometimes he would do this several times a night. Turner
would be so loud that he would wake up Red Dog. Red Dog
was a ten year old American Bulldog. Some think he may be a
pit bull, but no, he was a bull dog. His nickname was Boutros,
beautiful Boutros. Red Dog would wake up startled. He was the
family pet since the day he was born. Never aggressive towards
the family, but protective he was. Turner and Red Dog were like
brothers. They stayed together while Steve, Red Dogs owner,
and Mare were gone.

Mare's oldest daughter Geraldine would sometimes stay
with the dogs while they were gone. Steve was a thirty six year
veteran fireman engineer and Mare would be out occasionally
driving an eighteen wheeler. One time when Geraldine was
staying with the animals Turner and Red Dog had a fight
and Turner literally put Red Dogs head into his whole mouth.
Geraldine was horrified. Turner let the other animal go and Red
quickly retreated. Red Dog was very protective of his family.
He was often seen with his face sideways against the window
growling and teeth flashing. After the incident between the two
dogs Steve asked Mare to keep Turner outside in the kennel
until he became trustworthy again. The two animals never

again had an issue. Turner eventually came back in the house and the two were best of friends. These two had their antics that they pulled. They would sometimes escape the yard by different means. Red Dog would jump the five foot fence while Turner would lift the handle and walk through the gate. Their adventures would bring them home together several hours later or sometimes they would come home alone at different times. Regardless, these two dogs had a close bond.

Mare fell back to sleep, again around three am she was awakened by Turner growling. He was sitting up looking through the rear window of the camper shell. Mare saw nothing. She looked down towards the huge trash bins, still she could see nothing. Turner finally got quiet and fell back to sleep as did she.

SIX

ON THE THIRD DAY THE DAWN ROSE THROUGH THE FOREST WITH A slight chill. Mare made her usual tea and let Turner out to do his duties. That's when Mare saw it, a large elk peeking out from behind the thick brush. He was so beautiful. Once they made eye contact the elk sprinted away. Mare thought about how God made all the animals so beautiful and graceful. She drank her tea slowly while Turner quickly inspected the tree where the elk had been hiding. He smelled the roots, flowers, and the brush around the tree several times then must have decided that his hunger was more important. So he came and ate and slept some more.

The afternoon was eventful with another thunderstorm passing through. Mare had been busy arranging the back of the truck for Turner when the storm hit. She was trying to give him more room to lie down in during their travels. When the lighting cracked and thunder roared Turner had no issue of getting into the vehicle. With very little help from Mare he climbed right inside and waited out the storm. After the storm passed they went out for a little sightseeing. However, Mare did not realize that night came so quickly and they returned to their campsite for the evening as usual. Mare noticed upon their return that a lot of campers had left and saw two rangers drive by and waived. Turner, exhausted from his walk, ate his dinner and fell asleep for the night.

The evening of the third night was so dark, no lights illuminating the camp sites except for the light of the moon. Mare gazed at the stars; they were so big it looked like you could reach out and touch them. She had made a larger space for Turner in the bed of the truck and had both windows opened for him. He was sleeping comfortably now. Mares bed consisted of several large blankets piled high on her back seat with some pillows. She fell asleep as well. Turner woke Mare with his growling around one a.m. It was a very low growl and he was sitting up staring out the back window. He snorted a few times and Mare tapped on the window dividing the cab with the bed and told him to shut up. Finally Turner lay back down and Mare was closing her eyes to get back to sleep when she heard a heavy movement. Turner quickly sat up again and that's when Mare saw it; a huge shadow that she recognized immediately as a bear! Its head was four inches above her truck; standing on all four paws it stood motionless for a short time and then left. Mare was relieved; she fell asleep, but only for a minute or two. The bear came back and this time all hell broke loose! The bear weighing around 1100 to 1200 pounds was a grizzly; the bear bent down and poked its nose through the screen on the passenger side camper shell window. Turner was waiting there like a vulture. Once the bears nose and mouth were in the window Turner clamped down on it; a tug of war ensued. The bear was in shock, Turner was not letting go of his grip. He had a hold over the bear's mouth and held it shut tight. Turner was holding so tightly that when the bear tried to get away Turner dug his paws into the bed liner tearing out his toenails. The bear standing on all fours bellowed out deep roars echoing from the depths of its chest. Mare was in shock as the truck rocked back and forth, she was tossed from the front seat to the back and sideways. She said nothing but silently prayed that this would end soon. The bear seemed to become disoriented as it tried to pull out of the window, still Turner would not let go. Mare did not want to bring attention to her but quietly was telling Turner to let go. Finally after several minutes Turner let go of the bear. The grizzly took off squealing and whining like it was hurt. The rest of the night she stayed awake thinking that the bear might come back.

At dawn, Mare got out of the truck thinking it was probably safe to do so, started to look around. She was bleeding on her arms from being tossed around the vehicle and when she got to the side of her truck she saw blood and drool smeared along the side of it. Opening the back to check on Turner and let him out she saw that his feet were bleeding heavily and cried out. "Oh my Baby!" Panicking, she quickly wrapped his paws up and from what she could see he lost four of his toenails, one was still hanging precariously on his right rear paw. His face had a cut high up just below his right eye and he was mad, irritable, and quite aggressive. Mare proceeded with caution as she waited for the rangers to come out; they had some bandages for his feet. The rangers informed her that he needed veterinarian care and the nearest facility was in Jackson Hole, Wyoming, fifty miles south.

SEVEN

MARE BEING ANNOYED WITH THE SITUATION AND NEEDING TO DEAL with Turners injuries asked the rangers why a bear would even poke its head through the screen. They thought that maybe the bear thought Turner was cub since he closely resemble one already. This made some sense to Mare, but nevertheless she feared Turner would fall fatally if she did not get on the road to the veterinarians office. When she arrived, they took him in quickly; Turner was not a happy animal. The vet cleaned the wounds also removing the last hanging claw. After tending to Turners needs the veterinarian informed Mare that he might have a thyroid problem because of his large size. Mare just scoffed at the doctor. Due to his injuries Mare purchased a large ramp that allowed Turner to get in and out of the truck. He ended up losing four toenails including one dew claw. The rest of Turners nails needed to be trimmed. They had gotten so long that they were around and an inch and one fourth in length. However, Mare decided not to get them trimmed because she thought that he might need them that long while they were camping in Yellowstone and other forested areas.

They headed back to their campsite fifty miles north. Mare checked on Turner frequently. Once back in Yellowstone, she decided that sightseeing wasn't an option because there were too many people there now and Turner seemed to be developing a fever. She did take him to the geyser blow hole though. Once there she noticed that his feet were bleeding again and he had a lot of gunk in his eyes. After cleaning and tending to his feet they continued on up to Big Horn Mountain where there still was heavy snow on the ground. This gave Turner a great relief because the cold made his feet feel much better. Mare thinking how happy Turner was she felt great relief that he had almost become himself again. He ravaged the area, eating the snow and rolling around in it. He loved the snow! When it was time to go, Turner, carefully walked up the new ramp and got into the truck. Mare feared he was not as well as she thought. They left the area and went into Cody, Wyoming. She rented a motel room for the evening and this is where she heard about a large grizzly bear that had killed someone two days before Turners incident. She cringed at the very thought of it. Turners fever began to worsen and the gunk in his eyes continued as well. Mare beds him down as he did not eat his dinner; he tried but vomited up the food. She worried over him as he lay silent.

A knock at the door caught Mares attention. It was nearing the time for the big motorcycle ride to South Dakota. The couple in the next room asked Mare about the event and they marked it in their calendar. The husband was disabled from a motorcycle accident, but regardless, they were still attending the event. After some casual conversation the couple mentioned the story of the bear attack that they read in the local newspaper.

Mare told them about her and Turners experience as well. Word got around about Mare and Turner; most did not believe her until they saw Turner and his obvious injuries, this was no joke.

Turner seemed to be doing somewhat better the next morning, he tried to eat but the food did not stay down. As Mare was thinking about the fateful night that Turner fought off the bear a grave feeling came over her; a wounded bear loose in the forest and being a grizzly was a very dangerous prospect. She shuddered at the memory of the bear screaming in pain as it ran away into the forest. She silently prayed that no one else would encounter the grizzly bear.

In the forest along the icy waters rested a rather larger grizzly bear. It moaned slightly in pain, its face torn from the other animal. Slowly the bear arose and put its whole head under the icy water; the relief was most comforting. Relieved from the pain, the bear moved on looking for food. Weeks would pass before this bear would be completely healed.

EIGHT

DAYS PASSED ON AND TURNER GOT WORSE. THEIR DESTINATION WAS Nova Scotia but by the time Mare reached Vermont, Turner had become too ill to travel. Mare rented a room at a bed and breakfast where they stayed for three days. Mare knew that Turner needed further medical attention so she found a local veterinarian and took him there. Turner received eye cream, an anti-bacterial cream, and a spray for his feet. The doctor was so nice he gave Mare an ice chest full of ice packs to help keep Turner cool and relaxed. The doctor told Mare to use crazy glue on Turners toes to keep the bleeding from forming a shell around the bare skin. His feet were still in bad shape but this vet was great and he made Turner feel much better.

Mare wished there was a way to get Turner out of the heat and thought of putting him in the back seat of the truck. Turner having so much anxiety prevented that; driving with him right behind her would be a nightmare. He would thrash about and howl incessantly; he reminded Mare of a bull in the belly of a cattle wagon with all his heifers, screaming like a baby. As they started back towards Wyoming Turner began to change, his eyes became more like a bears as each day passed. The heat was taking its toll on Turner and his illness was getting worse. Mare would stop and let him out and Turner would be overcome by the heat, almost passing out. Mare thought about going to Canada, but with Turner sick like this they would never let him cross the border. The decision to cut the trip short returning west was somewhat of a heart break for her, but Mare had to do what was best for Turner. Then she thought of the Grizzly bear again. That night seemed to reenact itself over and over again, each time she shuddered. She thought about the minimal damage to the truck, only the screen being torn away and all of the slobber mixed with blood was starting to eat away the paint. They were lucky.

Mare met many people during their travels; it was a fun time for her. She really enjoyed the different types of people found in the different states. Turner met many breeds of dogs and other animals, some a little leery of him while others where very friendly. However, when it came right down to it, everyone was cautious around Turner. People still commented on how he looked like a bear because of his size and markings. Mare thought of the bear again; it preyed on her mind. Then she remembers a wounded grizzly is more dangerous than a thousand Chihuahuas singing in sync ready for the next chorus. Some people would say they would rather be around a bull mastiff than a pack of Chihuahuas. Mare believed it; but a wounded grizzly is the most deadly kind of creature.

Deep in the forest the large grizzly was now starting to heal. The mud pool packed about its wounds made for much comfort. As the bear lay quietly, eyes menacing and deadly, hunting its prey, spied upon an elk. Within seconds the bear had it down and began feasting on the meal. The roar of a fresh kill from a grizzly sent out signals all over the forest range. Wolves howled, buffalo skirted, and small animals fled to the safety of their habitat. Now full and content the bear left the carcass for scavengers to wage war over. The animals came in to get their piece of the meal and war ensued, even an Eagle swooped down to grab a chunk or two. In the end a mountain lion and her cubs carried off most of it. The bear had retreated to the mud pool and bathed in it as to relieve the pain from its wounds. The puncture wounds were deep and painful; any kind of relief would be soothing.

NINE

THERE WAS LOTS OF FLOODING IN VERMONT, NEW YORK, AND Pennsylvania – all across the North East regions. It was not only the heat that hit its highest in years on the Eastern seaboard; it was the flooding, extensive rain, and the tornadoes. Mare thought once she left the east she would be out of it. This thought proved not to be true. As they approach Indiana, Turner was in anguish, they stopped at a trucker's motel for a few days until he could travel again. He recovered fairly quickly but the fear in him was apparent as the storms raged outside, he would hide in the bathroom waiting for the thunder and lightning to pass.

Once they left Indiana they traveled quickly across Illinois and parts of Iowa trying to avoid coming head on with a F4 or F5 tornado. The warnings were everywhere and Mare decided to head north towards Iowa. The heat became quite humid and the wind was blowing up to eighty miles per hour in some areas. Finally on an old two lane road that Mare had driven years ago, they moved on. They reached Sioux Falls, South Dakota and all was quiet. Mare was thankful for making it there safely. Turner was overheated again and not doing well so she rented another room for the evening. With the air conditioner blowing right on him, Turner rested quietly on the bed.

The motel sat alongside of interstate 90; several motorcycles were traveling west and the road was very crowded due to the Fat Father of all motorcycle runs. People from all over the country came to South Dakota every August for this particular bike run. Mare smiled and thought how proud she was to be a small part of it all. She was planning to stop there and walk Turner through the vendor's booths before it opened. However, Mare did not get a chance to do this and the run was coming to a close. It was the fifth of August, 2011. Mare sat down wondering if she really had out run the tornadoes. The sky was getting very dark and Mare was concerned. She had turned on the television when she first arrived but now she started to watch; the ticker tape at the bottom of the screen warned of an impending tornado in the area where she had just come from. The news predicted winds to be around 160 mph and this storm would hit Sioux Falls around midnight or one in the morning; prediction is the tornado will be an F5.

The tornado finally developed and touched down in Oklahoma City then moved north destroying several homes in its path. Mare was saddened at the devastation and the effects this would have on the people. Deciding to take Turner out for one last bathroom break the sky lit up something fierce. It was around ten o'clock and the lighting was crackling across the sky in turning nighttime into day. Turner, afraid, quickly retreated to the motel room and hid in the bathroom in the tub. He made Mare laugh out loud because he looked so funny standing there.

Mare ate a small dinner afterwards and watched the rest of the news before going to bed. Just as she was finishing up late breaking news came across the screen and it said that in Big Horn Wyoming, a large grizzly was seen again by back packers, although it charged them, they managed to escape in their 4x4 vehicle. Mare was stunned, it had only been a few days since Turners encounter with the bear and now the same bears face is being flashed across the screen displaying the scars left by Turner. Mare shuddered knowing that the bear that attacked them is still out there, waiting. As Mare watched the news, she would freeze the television frame to study the bears face; noticing all the scars that Turner left behind. Going frame by frame on the TV set she tried to get an accurate size of the bear and wholly cow was he big. Big Bertha in Alaska was big but this guy was huge! Not even a match for two or three other grizzlies...gigantic!

The tornado was moving quickly across the state now and as the eleventh hour approached the weather man stated that it had changed course travelling in an easterly direction then turning north. They were fairly sure it would only skirt the outer rim of the city if at all. Mare lay down and called the hotel front desk to make sure they were safe and evacuations were not mandatory. They told her that the hotel was in a safe location. Turner was now sitting in the middle of the bathroom, his eyes like a bear, just waiting.

Around 1 am Turner started thrashing around the room wildly waking Mare from a peaceful sleep. He was in a panic! Mare got up to look outside and saw hail the size of golf balls falling from the sky, pounding down on here 4x4 truck.

Lightning streaked across the foreboding sky and the winds were furiously blowing. Mare took Turner outside because he was ramming the hotel door with his rear side, trying to escape. He tried to hide under a bush but Mare would not have it. As she was dragging him back into the room she look up and saw a large funnel cloud forming. Turner went straight back to the bathtub and hid again, he was terrified. Suddenly the lights went out and it seemed like the world just stopped which added to the fear as the eye of the tornado was directly overhead. The funnel retreated back to the ominous sky and the roar became deafening so much that Mare was covering her ears as she hid with Turner in the bathtub together. Scared to death they stayed in there huddled together for more than an hour. Finally around three in the morning light rain began to fall and Mare felt it was safe to get out of the tub but Turner would not budge.

Mare went to the window and looked outside seeing that the truck was ok and the town was still there. Lightning could still be seen off in the distance and their motel lights had come back on. Exhausted, Mare finally went to bed. During the rest of the night thunder came and went, Turner remained in the tub and several small tornadoes had touched down all over the place. Mare packed up and left, no use in trying to sleep. The lack of sleep reminded her of the night she tried to sleep after the bear attack, it wasn't possible.

TEN

MARE TRAVELLING DOWN THE INTERSTATE WAS FEELING DISAPPOINTED to not be able to make their destination of Nova Scotia; another place another time she thought. Turner was in the back of the truck and seemed to be feeling better as they travelled. Mare thought about his brave soul and how he always fought to protect her and how he seemed to know her every move. She imagined him thinking to himself how he fought that grizzly, flattering himself, and then thinking how if there was a next time he would fight to the death. Turner laid down, Mare relaxed as she drove towards Big Horn Mountain. She was trying to get there before nightfall however, Turner made a turn for the worse, his illness was back upon him and his eyes became like that of a bear, dark and menacing. Mare let him out to get some air but the heat was so crushing it overtook him and they hurried on their way reaching Wyoming and rented a cabin in Buffalo. They continued on their journey until they reached the town of Big Horn where Turners most recent veterinarian was located. They took such good care of him and the vet seemed to just love Turner. This vet was different from the normal ones because not only did she treat dogs and cats, but goats, pigs, and chickens were at the hospital. It was like a farm. Turner had contracted a bacterial infection from the bear he fought with and the infection had been lingering making him sick. After many tests and talk, the vet treated Turner for the infection, thyroid problems, and the beginning of dehydration. Turner had to take lots of medicine and get a few shots. He wasn't very happy about this.

During the week they stayed in Big Horn Mare had learned that Turners tale with the bear was becoming quite well known around town. The people were very friendly and the cabin she stayed in was nice too. Word travelled fast in a small place like that and everyone seemed to be worried about Turners health. He was not out of the woods yet, the veterinarian kept a close watch on his conditions. He was still not able to keep his food down.

As Mare rested one evening and Turner laid on the bed like he owned it, the news came on and started to report about a hiker who had been on a designated trail was charged by a rather large grizzly bear; the hiker dropped his pack and ran away terrified of the event. Another hiker some ways off was able to shoot a video of the bear and was astonished at the size of this guy. The face was a close up and on its face were identical scars as the one Turner fought with. The video showed the bear growling and as soon as Turner heard that he was up from the bed and staring at the television; Mare could see in his eyes he was remembering that night. Turner growled really low, almost like he was pulling the pits of hell out from Earth. The announcer continued saying that all hikers and campers should be aware that this guy is lingering and to be careful. Not worth losing one's life.

Turner laid down to rest so Mare went out to enjoy the BBQ with the people near the pool. As she shared the meal she sensed Turner awakening so she returned to the cabin. As she entered the room he was in the center of the room, his eyes blacked as coal, stared at the television again because the news was replaying the bear video. Agitated, Turner peed on the carpet and growled continuously. Mare quickly took him outside and tethered him to a tree. Shutting off the television she hoped that would be the last she ever saw of that bear again.

As their time in Big Horn passed, Turner became well again and Mare decided it was time to start their journey again. She had enjoyed her time there immensely, swimming every day, seeing a parade, and doing some light shopping, it was just what she had needed. Turner was not bleeding on his feet anymore, nor was he sick to his stomach, so much better they began to prepare for the trip ahead.

The cabin owners showed Mare how to fold the back seat of her truck and make a bed for Turner who would be much more comfortable there. So she put everything else in the back of the bed and packed the bags planning on her departure early the next morning. Turner was much happier and lively since he was on his proper medications now. No more laziness or being faint, he was active and had lost weight too. It was time to go; they were both ready.

ELEVEN

Back on the road against heading north to Montana, Mare stopped at many small towns looking for a place to live but nothing was of interest to her. One man told her to go to North Dakota that it seems like everyday someone becomes an instant millionaire with all the oil in the state. Mare contemplated the idea only because she knew he wasn't lying, she had heard the same thing on the local news. She decided to go back to her starting point, that is Big Bear, California.

The news once again was reporting more bear attacks. This time it was near the Wyoming – Montana border, the northwestern forest near Yellowstone National Park. With this news she shuddered and hoped that it was not the same bear. It had been nearly six weeks since Turner had his tug-o-war encounter with the grizzly. She spent another night in the motel.

Working over her finances Mare was realizing how much time her and Turner had actually spent in motels; it was a bit overwhelming. Now in the second week of August the rains came heavily in Montana, Mare just smiled thinking about Mother Nature and how nice it was to be in a room out of the rain. Turner woke ad ate his dinner while she continued contemplating where to go. Even though she said she would go back to California, Alaska had always called out to her but to no avail she would not venture that way this year. So somewhat disheartened she turned the television to catch the news and once again a grizzly was sighted northwest of the Montana still somewhat close to Yellowstone. Although it travelled alone the bear had attacked and killed several deer, sheep, and other animals along its journey. Farmers were being warned to be on the lookout for the grizzly and Mare began to fear knowing that the killer was still out there. She decided to get an early start the next morning and to drive an old route which she had not been on in years. As sleep came to her she was still thinking about the route and how it was the back way to Yellowstone; away from people and the bear. Sleep overtook her quickly and morning was upon her before she knew it. Eager and ready to go they both started their journey back to California. Turner munched on a muffin and maple bar and Mare laughed as she watched him enjoy has food. Looking at an approaching sign she asked Turner if he was ready to cross the border know what happened last time they came through this part of the country. He was fast asleep.

As she drove through Wyoming she knew exactly where she was except that she thought the left turn should have been a right, oh well, it will end up at the trucker's entrance anyways. Lots of buffalo here, at least there was 25 years ago. Off she went left then right, the road turned to a solid packed dirt road about an hour into the trip; still there were lots of trees and foliage. The road started to get smaller, not winder, she remembered that two eighteen wheelers could not really pass each other on the straight part of the road. Hmm. Her mind was wondering about her daughters in California, and if maybe she could stay with Adelaide until she found a new place in Big Bear? She would call later when they took another break. Looking around at the scenery while driving she noticed that the springs of fresh water had been stolen away by the underground volcanic activity here. The cell phone rang, Mare quickly answered but the phone fell from her hands. Retrieving the phone had wakened Turner, it was around noon and half the day was gone. Mare pulled into the parking area and let Turner out; she did not tether him.

TWELVE

IN THE FOREST THE LARGE GRIZZLY BEAR HAD FINALLY HEALED. THE
bear was scarred but all his pain had subsided. He stood up
listening, hearing nothing he dropped to all four paws. Again
a faint sound aroused his curiosity; he stood up again listening
intently. In the distance four trappers and rangers were waiting
for him. Their intent was to put him down and do it quickly.
The bear had been attacking all too often and over a wide range.
Two hikers approached completely unaware of the grizzly. The
rangers lying in wait saw the hikers and got them off the trail.
A black bear cub came down the trail on its own merry way,
but this was not the bear they awaited. The grizzly aware of
the smaller cub and its mother took shelter behind a large tree,
now out of sight of the rangers and the unsuspecting cub. The
mother bear not far behind approached her cub and stood up
listening, she was nowhere the size of the beast that waits to
catch his prey. She dropped to all four paws hugging her cub
close by. Still off in the distance were the rangers and hikers
waiting silently for something to happen. This time it was the
grizzly's turn to make a move.

Turner looked at Mare; he quickly took off tracking the area smelling every little spot and nook in the ground. He smelled the bear, horrible like the sites for garbage dumps. Turner quickly disappeared into the forest; they were in an isolated part rarely used by anyone. Mare took the opportunity to keep talking to Adelaide. Mare started to call Turner but he really was gone, no response from him at all. Adelaide is still talking on the phone asking if Mare would pet sit when she got back in town so that Adelaide could take a quick weekend trip to Las Vegas. Mare's prayers were answered; she had a place to stay. While her conversation continued, Turner was out investigating the smells that attracted him. Adelaide hung up and Mare was wondering where Turner was off too. Mare went to get out of the truck to look for him when suddenly she heard a loud roar!

The rangers were still waiting for him, an hour had passed. They thought maybe they had lost the bear even after they had spread out to cover more area. He could have slipped away unnoticed. Just when they thought it was clear to stand up there behind them only a few feet away stood the largest grizzly they had ever seen; charging at them full speed! The mother bear and cub had escaped to a large cave unbeknownst to the grizzly. However, the ranger, trappers, and hikers were running for their lives. The grizzly was showing no sign of slowing; his intentions were to kill these people. In the trees stood silently watching the beast chase the humans was Turner. His eyes like the bear, completely black and filled with a hatred for this grizzly; he remained hidden. The people had found a hiding place and thought it might be clear to leave, so they stood up, and the bear saw them charging towards them once again. In an instant Turner flew out of the trees and in the air like a grand eagle seeking his prey hit the bear full force just above its humped neck. The force took the grizzly by surprise yet continued charging towards the people. Turner rebounded and again leapt towards the bear and hit the bear just below his neck area causing the bear to fall. The bear tried to regain its balance but was caught off guard by an empty well that he stumbled and fell down into. A well that had been part of a series of geysers in the area but now was dry. The silence was deafening. Turner stood at the edge of the well and looked down. It looked as if he was smiling, he defeated his enemy. No more would he have to worry about this bear with the facial scars haunting his memories.

Turner eyed Mare as she came through the trees looking for him. The rangers and others came out of their hiding places relieved to see what had just transpired. They looked at Turner and told Mare he had just saved their lives! What a hero! Surprised they looked down the well to see such a magnificent animal lying dead and forever silenced at the bottom of the well, the moment so surreal. Mare said to the rangers "Kinda reminds me of a deadfall, doesn't it?" They just looked her and then once again at the bear. It would be several days before the rangers could climb down to examine the carcass and they had to decide to leave it to nature or remove it. Either way, Mother Nature had her way and the cycle of life will continue. The grizzly was dead and the fear was over.

THIRTEEN

FINALLY HAPPY TO BE HEADING HOME AND SUCH A WEIGHT LIFTED, they left the group of people after hugs and pictures were taken. Turner was going to be in the local newspaper. Mare and Turner trudged back to the truck through the thick foliage and Mare thought how Mother Nature can change things so much. Whether it's the road or the bear, nature has its own power to control the environment and the life that exists within her.

Back at the truck they loaded up and Mare put away her shotgun. They were off. She passed through the gates one more time and Mare thought how nice it was that they could go that way just one more time. They made it out of the park and to a motel for the evening. It was so nice to be able to sleep and not hear the faint sound of a bears roar. Turner slept quite soundly. The next day was a fisherman's competition so they had to leave very early. This was good for them because Mare arrived at Adelaide's that next evening. Happy to see them, Adelaide barbecued steaks and they enjoyed conversation with the kids, and pets. Mare was going to pet sit all these animals... Turner, the bear killer; Rambo, a German Shepard; Coco, a

Chihuahua; Cobra, a very mellow cat; and Red Dog, an ancient red nosed bull dog. All the animals had their issues getting along, but they eventually did and when Adelaide returned from her trip Mare took Turner and Coco to a cabin in Sugarloaf. Coco and Turner had become best friends.

Turner eventually healed from all of his injuries. His face had healed but his skin was so leathery is reminded Mare of the bear and his toe nails did grow back but turned white. He lies on his quilt and falls asleep quickly; nothing to wake him, the world just passing by as he rests. The jest of this story is the bear doesn't always win, especially if he fights a Sheriff dog named Turner.

The End

EPILOGUE

The moral of this story remains in the hands of today's society. With its crumbling walls of destruction against humanity, loss of jobs, homes, money, healthcare to say the least, leaves us humans nowhere to go except to the safety of our mountain forest. Looking for a place to homestead, a piece of land, to save and raise our families on. All the while, entering the no zone, the habitat of safety for all species of animals, who have never known such terror or invasion on such a large scale go on without a whisper giving their lives, as we humans become the predators.

Ask yourself this question:

Are you a predator stalking your prey or have you become the prey?

Our most treasured gift-THE ANIMAL KINGDOM!

BE ANIMAL AWARE

M.E. BLAZIC

ABOUT THE AUTHOR

Now retired living in Alaska has decided to pursue the career they started years ago. Being a writer is a hard task not to be taken lightly. This writer intends to recapture those years, along with you my most valued reader.

Printed in the United States
by Baker & Taylor Publisher Services